My Favorite Failures

My Favorite Failures

Andy Roberts

Half Inch Press

© Andy Roberts 2025

ISBN 978-1-969849-02-2

All rights reserved. No part of this book may be reproduced or transmitted in any manner without author's written permission.

Contents

Diagnosis 1
Leaning Toward Greenland 3
Search for Life on the Ohio River 5
Parsimony 7
Empty Rooms 8
Celebration 9
Swineherd 10
IH 11
Child Bride 13
Gravel Road 14
Stroke Dance 15
Mechanic 16
Osmosis 17
Seized by the Notion 18
Still Preying 19
Just Visiting 20
Obituaries over Coffee 21
hootenanny 22
Blind Faith 23
Graveyard Shift 24
Half Past December 25
Hawk and Cop 26
Kinship 27
Youth 28
Mobile Home 29
The Cage 30
Luxury 32

Jerry and Amy	33
Little Phrase from Brahms	34
Leonard and I	35
Pareidolia	36
Wolf Circles the Dream	37
Juniper Jones	38
Giant	39
quaaludes and cuervo	40
Nadine	41
Never Enough	42
Tammy Wynette Blues	43
Sixty	44
The Healer	45
Sodbuster	46
Gentle on My Mind	47
Stage Fright	48
Plasma	49
Winter Solstice	51
He Swears He Sees	52
McClenney to Beeville	53
Buttermilk Johnson	54
Paychecks and Fish Heads	55
Late Winter Blues	57
Sizzler	58
It's Raining at the Birthplace of Ulysses S. Grant	59
Late Night Poem	60
Open Mic	61
Crepuscule with Bourbon and Cigar	63

Diagnosis

Another old-fashioned rain
and whiskey leaks
through the broken brown stumps
of my teeth.

The fact
I've got nothing to lose
but my life
is a comfort.

9:00 pm and the glass
is half full.
"Love Hurts"
by Boudleaux Bryant,

who wrote six thousand songs,
and all night long
the wind's been looking
for what it's lost.

Lately
it seems like
everyone my age
looks older than me.

Time has reduced me
to shaving by feel,
my parents still hard at work
in my blood cells.

10:00 pm and the radio plays
Taylor Swift's acoustic version of
Tool's "Stinkfist."
The world has gone wrong.

But I've got my whiskey
and the whole night to kill.

Red Sovine's "Teddy Bear"
and "Giddy Up Go."

My tastes are catholic.
I love the dead
because it's way easier
than emotional honesty.

"Bonnie and Clyde" on TCM.
Bonnie writes a poem
that gets published
in the local paper.

Clyde is proud,
and the banjo plays
"Foggy Mountain Breakdown."
They'll both be dead in twenty minutes.

Live fast and leave
a good looking corpse
didn't work out for me.
In the future

only the poor
will die ugly.
Six thousand shell casings
and roll credits.

The rain has stopped.
The movie's over.
Earth lurches forward
into uncertainty.

The homeless street preacher
who told me
You'll never see God with your eyes,
downs a goblet of Thorazine.

Leaning Toward Greenland

A man on the radio tells me
"It's never too early for nostalgia."
Greenland, I learn, has a suicide rate
six times higher than the world's average.
More cheery news: I have a full pack of cigarettes
but no lighter. Also,
there are no psychiatrists in Greenland,
but fifty-six social workers.

My thoughts lean toward Greenland
when the temperature nudges ninety.
We've just notched the warmest year in living memory,
yet the climate change deniers persist.
The planet wobbling on its axis
like a top losing velocity.
Napa Valley grapes shrivel into raisins
while Palm Desert's fairways glisten like emeralds
arranged on parchment for billionaires.
A zen garden for meditation on pork belly futures.

Touching on nostalgia, I remember
one cold summer in Sault Ste. Marie the locals referred to
as three months of bad sledding.
And we walked to school, back and forth,
but not uphill, both ways.

The ice cubes are melting in my Wild Turkey.
Bourbon is a drink best enjoyed in February.
Gin is a summer drink but unfortunately
tastes like perfume, Chanel No. 5, I've tried them both.

I find my lighter in the junk drawer
beneath three pairs of scissors, two cell phone chargers,
a roll of surgical tape and a spray of forgotten business
      cards.
On the back of Bear's Small Engine Repair,
my handwriting: *God gave her*

a nose for cocaine, a face to find the fist.
I flip it over, notice Bear lives
on 194 Barbarian Street.

It's time to turn the radio off,
smoke my American Spirit on the patio
with the lights off,
see if I can spot any stars
burning through the world's pollution.

Search for Life on the Ohio River

I abandon the checkbook in disgust,
head out in the Honda, all windows open
in the death of December,
hotheaded, teary-eyed, hit ninety
to find something approaching peace of mind.
Slow down, look around.
One thousand men eating mashed potatoes,
all up and down the Ohio River,
losing teeth, one at a time.

I take the road north and discover
music at an empty rest stop,
melodies established with three notes.
These from small brown birds
who suffer terribly in the cold,
but hang on with numb feet to the wire
and continue singing.

Up and down the river I search
for life and find it
in the plainest places.
A killer sugar pie recipe
from a pregnant grandmother at Rooster's.
A one-armed mechanic in Marietta
who welds tight my cracked exhaust manifold
as I wait in his tin-roofed garage close to the kerosene
       heater.
A junkie at an NA meeting
who shows me how to
crush my oxy beneath a dollar bill,
roll the single for a straw.

I make my way back
to the checkbook, of course.
Practical, always practical.

Nose, a dollar bill dusted

with the fine residue of oxy.
Couple of loose teeth.

Parsimony

Parsimony I learned from my grandfather
on my father's side who owned an aircraft
in the Depression but burned tires for heat,
and beat his wife for her beauty which drove him
mad with jealousy and never washed his clothes
but layered them over dirt. Who could fix anything
with pinchers and baling wire but graduated
to duct tape and never ate pizza but had a taste
for mullet though they were well known as trash fish.
He was still alive in 1983 when he met
my Korean wife and whispered in my ear:
Does she eat with them sticks? Is she Christian?
This was the way he survived: one meal a day
at the Sizzler and sleeping it off all afternoon.
He and his fourth wife lost my father
to the Children's Home of Springfield Ohio,
Irish Hill, where they boiled their cabbage,
collected cigarette ends. At the age of ten
my father set pins at Galaxy Bowl and
fractured an eye socket you couldn't set,
cut his own switch for his daily beatings.
His habits were hardwired.
A toothpick to hold his cigar butt
and the cheapest beer money could buy.
The Coast Guard taught my father all he ever
needed to know, the secret to becoming
one squared away individual which worked
beautifully solo, a family another matter.
Which explains my writing on both
sides of the paper and using scraps and counting
my money each night to fall asleep.

Empty Rooms

A janitor at Beaches Hospital,
I helped the Filipino maids clean the rooms
when a patient died. The maids wouldn't.
They'd cry and shake, absolutely refuse.
Death didn't bother me.
I'd go in with my dustmop, wet mop,
clean the floor, empty the trash.
"See," I'd say. "No ghosts."
I'd strip the sheets off the bed.
Eventually the maids would return.
We'd turn the tv on and finish cleaning.

I'd gotten to know the patients who died,
chit-chatted with them every morning
while cleaning their rooms,
for weeks, months even.
Then they'd die and I'd be stripping the sheets off,
joking about ghosts.

Fifty years ago, and the way
I handled things still bothers me.
I could have done better,
shown more respect.
Maybe joking about ghosts
was my version of
whistling past the graveyard.
I think about those empty rooms,
more and more now –
the way I handled things –
the closer I get
to filling one of the beds.

Celebration

> Jacksonville Beach 4th of July 1976

I walked the hardpacked sand at 9:00 pm
with the Camaros and pickup trucks with huge tires
backed up toward the boardwalk, the young
seated on hoods sipping Schlitz Malt Liquor,
holding hands, kissing, stereos competing.
Kliegs over the boardwalk cast shadows and light,
filling faces of the milling crowd
with Toulouse-Lautrec-like hues and angles.
Thousands old and young wandered,
waving lighted sparklers in figure eights, contrails.
Red cigarette ends raised to chicken-footed puckers,
bottle rockets, machinegunning strings of firecrackers.
I roamed the beach, wondering what was wrong:
the drugs, the occasion or me.

I kept walking and the lights began to fade,
the crowd to thin. I could make out
snatches of songs from the parked F-150's,
"Cross-Eyed Mary," "Tangled Up in Blue,"
smell the dope.

Then it was dark, no more cars.
Fireworks burst over the boardwalk pier
and the crowd cheered like the sound of a football game
far away. To the north
I could see lights of the Atlantic Beach hotels
and walked toward them,
where I would turn inland and head home.

The sound of small waves crashing and washing back,
so quiet I could hear the bubbles,
little pieces of sand and shell dragged back.
I smiled there in the dark, enjoying the celebration
at last.

Swineherd

You could tell by the hands
and the way he prayed
over his small bowl of mixed vegetables
at lunch in the cafeteria,
everyone else eating pizza,
doughnuts and carrot cake.
We were maids and maintenance men.
Charles Freeman was a janitor,
with huge hands to pray
over a small bowl of succotash.
You would have thought he came from another world.
We could place him in his long dark robe
and perfectly trimmed beard.
Kneeling down to pray, lowering his forehead
three times a day and the anger in his eyes,
the slight crease in his perfect clothes.
We could see through him and our sympathy passed
through our hands to his small dark wife
as we touched her bruises, dried the water in her eyes.
We could see him on the back of his beast,
hear the long switch slicing through dusty air,
the cries of his herd and his curses.
It was the same man, the same man everywhere,
controlled by his ideas of order.

III

The old men who worked there were in their forties,
crippled by manual labor, poisoned by paint fumes –
they were drunks to make sense of it, to live with it.
They made a truck, their last gasp, we had one –
a 1968 Travelall with three rows and a wayback,
no seat belts, AM radio, three on a tree.
Everyone in Springfield worked there
as long as they could stand it.
Dad made it three years,
Grandma thirty. She died of cancer
at sixty, Dad at fifty. Dead drunks.
I learned to drive in the Travelall
with bad clutch, vinyl seats, huge mirrors.
The smell of the heater was popcorn and
cigarettes, December. I remember Nat King Cole,
the Rolling Stones' "Satisfaction."
Willie Woods, Juvenile Delinquent of 1967,
smashed the windshield with a brick one summer.
Police never caught him, but he died
of a heroin overdose, his slicked back hair
in the newspaper. I cracked my window
to get fresh air, sucking in oxygen to escape
the smoke, and they laughed at my gasping fish lips.
I could read road signs before anyone else
could see them, we made a game of it
and I won, blurting *Ashtabula 32 Miles*.
I never worked on the line, they shut it down
before I graduated. Dad joined the Coast Guard
for $88 dollars a month, free housing,
a chance to see the world.
I don't know why he bought the International,
it was a terrible vehicle with bad clutch,
popcorn, cigarettes, mirrors.
Everyone in Springfield died making the Travelall –
the fumes, the drinking, the crippled crawling

down the sidewalks with their pension checks
falling from their pockets, their eyes on fire,
inflamed with anger, love for the shoddy product.

Child Bride

After Jim Harrison's "God's Mouth"

My fingers are turning brown again,
though with tobacco not weed,
and my mother doesn't sew the seed
burns in my shirts anymore and never asks why.
She never searched my sock drawer where she
would have found the twenty-dollar lids for sale.
Mom raised me with benign neglect, a form of permissive
        parenting,
though truthfully she didn't have a clue, being a child
        herself.
Her only goal a happy offspring.

But now I have pity and perspective and an unexpected
source of happiness sliding in and out like clouds over sun.
Even the prospect of God is not so daunting.
Jim Harrison tells a story about a huge African catfish
who gathers her babies in her mouth
when danger lurks: they can swim in and out.
Mom named me after two saints and hoped
I would become a man of faith.
She knows I'm in the mouth
sometimes now and sometimes out.

Gravel Road

I used to walk home from school
down the long gravel road
behind Shakey's Pizza.
To pass the time,
I'd pretend I was blind.
Close my eyes,
see how long I could go
before my shoes scuffed grass.

I didn't know any blind people
then. Still don't. Except for
one very old woman
who can make out large print
held right up close to her glasses.

That road behind Shakey's Pizza
led to a trailer and a bedroom window
not thirty feet from a railroad line.
All night long trains used to crash
and smash open my sleep
until one day they just didn't.

What I'm saying is, I'm beginning
to understand how things work out
over a long period of time.
The old blind woman knows
I can't read small print anymore.
I walk carefully down stairs
with a firm grip on the handrail.
Have to take my medicine or die.
A kid playing blind to pass the time
down that long road to
learning you get used to things
one train wreck at a time.

Stroke Dance

Once off the crutches
my father walks like a dog with a broken spine,
moving in slow circles, desperate to please,
speech a series of barks and whines,
tapping the tip of his cane in code,
a morse for narcotics.

Dressed in pajamas he performs
his nightly dance for approval
down the hospital hallway,
brightly painted cane a carved root
from the Caribbean, tapping a music
slow and thick as the tongue in his head.

Mechanic

Jimmy Roberts was mad for speed.
Never left the farm, except for
summer afternoons at three thousand feet,
over cornfields in the crop duster
he rebuilt with pinchers and baling wire.

Fix anything with a motor.
Tear it down, bore it out, grease it up.
Jimmy Roberts, The Barney Oldfield of
Springfield, Ohio. Eighty years
he spun his wheels over town,
the hearts of Clark County gals.

Chased Evelyn as she rode the bus to work
every day for two months straight,
leaning out the window, hands off the wheel,
clutching his heart, pouring out
"Heaven, I'm in heaven. And my heart beats
so fast that I can hardly stand it."

Until one day she stepped off the bus,
into the passenger seat of his V-8 Ford.
Bonnie and Clyde until Dad's head crowned.
Lost him to the Children's Home,
then the marriage.

Jimmy Roberts broke down anything with
moving parts, family included.
Burned them up, tore them down,
beat them for their beauty.
Over cornfields he roared,
eyes on fire, redlining dials,
throttling the stick like the lives
he couldn't fix.

Osmosis

What to do was a question
I solved every afternoon
with two joints to burn the energy,
leave the question in mind where
it gleaned the day's events
through process of osmosis.

Story was all.
The boy with hydrocephalus,
the coven of witches I delivered a pizza to,
David Walters who called himself Purple Eagle,
lived in a tipi in his parents' back yard.

I still use that system though
I no longer own a Rottweiler,
a Harley, and a furious metabolism.

The American Interstate killed my friends,
then the needle and bottle.
I absorbed their lives through
the skin, my blood barrier, their stories
under my tongue, sublingual,
whatever you want to call the process
used to keep them all alive.

Seized by the Notion

Johnny Cash on the turntable,
straight razor and a bottle of
Wild Turkey. They all came today
in a package from a friend
whose motives remain debatable.
I've tried all three. With whiskey
laced spit I shave a little patch
bare on my left forearm,
Cash intoning "The Ballad of Ira Hayes."
Don't know if it's the lyrics,
bite from the first hit off the bottle
or something else that brings
the tears to my eyes.
I'm thinking of that commercial
about pollution, Iron Eyes Cody
watching all the trash blow around him,
a single tear hanging in his left eye.
Suddenly I'm seized by the notion
of finishing the bottle by noon,
having a shave.
I've always wondered
what kind of a man gets
falling down drunk at 10:00 am.

Still Preying

A man named Peter Popoff
promises a check for $56,000.00
and two ounces of magic spring water,
which will solve all your problems,
provided you send in a small donation.
This man owns a face with two eyes,
a mouth like a horrible hole
cut in a pancake.

All these years after Oral Roberts,
Little Jimmy Bakker, men like
Peter Popoff still prey on the man
who'll lay down his last twenty on a 40 ounce,
a bag of chips and a handful of scratch-offs.
Millions who lead lives unimaginable
to the dentist, mayor, banker.
A world of payday lenders, title loans,
utility shutoffs, bill collectors.

The mayor of Pleasantville doesn't understand:
these men at the Mini-Mart see themselves
as temporarily disappointed millionaires.
They want no part of collective good citizenship,
some democratic ideal of income equality.
They're going to hit it rich.
And it's only a matter of time
till their numbers add up.

Just Visiting

I was lost in the '40's for twenty years.
Sharp clothes and heroin. I found some comfort there.
I was born against my will, like every actor on earth.
But I'm in no hurry to leave
my sip of black coffee and crisp white shirts.
That's how it is sometimes when the world is off your back:
like Jean-Paul Belmondo and Jean Seberg in bed.
Although he died, of course. Shot in the back.

It's forty degrees and raining this early November
        afternoon,
all the leaves dropped off the trees. Sometimes I find
such beauty in the dead.
The clean white bones of the world in my teeth.
Nothing to do but watch the storm roll over
the prairie, listen for thunder.

It's raining harder now, wind lashing
limbs against the window and what's this
good time doing in my head?
I thought I was sick. It's probably
just visiting but I wish it would stay awhile.

Obituaries over Coffee

Old guys with names like Bud, Lou and Walt.
Young guys with names like Colt, Ridge and Pine.
A girl named Medusa Hightower,
her brothers Cyclops, Onan and Oedipus,
from Mayor's Income, Tennessee.
Every day, people younger than me are dropping.
Women live longer than men.
Writing of a child's death is shorter than its life,
too terrible to comprehend.
The world is so cruel we invented gods,
cultivated flowers.

hootenanny

we made machines of rosewood spruce and maple
battled fascists in guthriespeak at hootenannies
little dab of dippity do you remember elvis nat king
too many vicks inhalers did a number on the stomach
cheap and legal flying was the order of the man said
ask not what your country can do but why not join
the peace corps bring the big bucks can do
bag a rice or two when nikita did the shoe
che went bananas and what's that got to do with
michael row your boat ashore so peter paul and mary
puffed a magic dylan did a kingston if you don't shave
or get a haircut son we didn't send you to college
to be a bum we sang in rosewood bark and wormwood
bite grooving finger tips a hat to woody did the
dust bowl ballads rambling jack and bobbie
beat the stuffing out of fascists with a wood machine

Blind Faith

In Arles they found him without a hat
striding through stinkweed, wet to the knees,
no dog to cheer him. A raven followed,
harassing, pecking at his ears.
This was a blind Jesus with
brutal thumbs, huge nose, tiny broken teeth
they worshipped in the Kingdom of the Franks
after the Moderns, the Primitives, a pale bloody savior.
This Christ never rested but churned like a locomotive,
red coal in his pipe a pilot light
guiding those who followed.
Devotion a joke to the jealous,
whose jeers started as whispers,
veering into laughter, insults.
When he tamed the crow it perched on his shoulder,
soothing, clucking, waiting for the opportunity
to peck out the right eye, then the left.
But the savior flinched at the last second,
unable to complete the scarification.
Onward he steamed, chewing the wheat, charging,
boots broken, blood drying on his face in the hot sun,
wind whipping, knocking him down, stumbling onward,
sight swirling through cypresses, cornfields.
They loved him for inventing the sunflower,
for planting it there, in the south of France,
hands plunged in black dirt, nails jammed with it,
the only thing blind his faith in the good strong light.

Graveyard Shift

Laura Cobb, tall and grim
like her pale, tattooed father
who sold me Michelob and Zig-Zags
at the 7-11 on 3rd Street.

I was fifteen, same as Laura, who liked me,
but was going steady with an older guy.
Dirk drove a Camaro with a hood full of flames,
Goodyear slicks. Wore a fringed buckskin jacket,
muttonchops, large wallet
attached by a chain to his beltloop.
Knew I couldn't compete
with that kind of maturity.

Laura and I never kissed.
But our conversations were easy,
as we shared a joint before English.
Laura was comfortable with boys and men,
easy like how her father took my money for a six-pack,
handed me the Zig-Zags instead of
dropping them in the bag with the beer.
Loved how Laura said "cool" when I lit the joint,
blew me a shotgun
on her first hit.

Dirk with his fringe, chained wallet,
muttonchops, Camaro.
Laura's old man, pale and grim,
faded tattoos snaking up forearms.
I was scared.
Laura was going places
I wasn't ready to visit.
Her future flashing
in her old man's eyes.

Half Past December

Sky spitting snow as I cup my hands
around a Bic at 9:00 pm,
thinking how my cousin Jack the junkie
did it with his Zippo.
How he slept under the table last Christmas,
his mother pleading "Wake up, sleepyhead."
His pale bruised arms a horrible sight.

Just over one year sober –
until, weighing boredom against risk –
I choose the more interesting option.
Crushed oxy dripping down my throat,
bitter taste I love.
I'm a smart user.
Lie flushing my face
hot enough to melt snow.

Desire is the source of all sorrow.
What good does this knowledge do me?
I'm still alive but only
because I'm scared of needles.

Hawk and Cop

In Chester, West Virginia,
wife visiting a friend,
I'm wasting time by
walking railroad tracks.
Bend down to touch steel rails
warmed by March sun.
No one around except for one cop,
who slows down to examine my behavior.

I turn over a dead starling with my stick.
Pick up a dead ladybug, weightless
as I bounce it in my palm.
Look east to the Alleghenies.
Wind's knife slits eyes shut.
Red hawk circling thermals.

Hawk and cop watching
every move.
Decide to head back
to the house.
Feeling like a cotton tail,
a white-tailed deer,
an unhoused human
with no ID.

Kinship

Emmetsburg, Iowa 1885: a home
on the floodplain, a fire to
stare into, tend the iron pot.
Where my great great grandfather Spear wrote
in a spidery hand with a pen cut from a turkey feather:
Damn this mud straight to hell!

Stuck in the Iowa sod spinning his wheels.
Nothing but black dirt as far as he could see.
The long leather belts of his thresher
turning slowly enough to watch corn dust
rise in still air, a single kernel ride the wave,
huff and belch of steam a music too slow for his ears.

It was speed he was mad for,
the internal combustion engine.
Whiskey only slowed him down.
Useless when fiddles did that fraying thing
with horsehair burning –
it was laudanum that did the trick.

Looking out my kitchen window
at the bare branch of a hackberry tree.
Born in the wrong century, Spear and I.
No fire to tend. No iron pot. No laudanum.
When my wheels are spinning, when hair is burning,
I attack the keys of my plastic computer:

I need knee-deep black Iowa mud!
Give me the great, dented face
of the anvil to bang on.
Jam black dirt deep beneath my nails.
Free me from the curse of the 21st century
disease of digital ennui.

Youth

Curtis Massey is nine years old.
Gregg Allman hair and a red
mouth that hangs open,
says nothing.

Curtis Massey on a swing
in the park at night
hanging out with teenagers.

His mother is dead and he lives
with his three older brothers who
pass him joints, feed him acid.

As the swing descends,
Curtis Massey passes the joint
to his right.

The swing squeaks
as the joint
makes the rounds.

None of them want
more than they've got
right now.

Moonlight,
a few leaves left
on the oak tree
above.

Mobile Home

A certain type of bad luck
permeates life in a mobile home.
Your car will break down.
Your children will turn to drugs.
Your wife will leave you.
You'll lose your job.
Your heart will attack you.
Your dog will die.
A roach will float in your bathtub.
You'll buy Raid and the cheapest cigarettes
money can buy.
You'll order pizza and frequent
Golden Corral and Chinese buffets.
Your loan application will get rejected.
Your tags will expire.
Your girlfriend will sell your guitar for crack.
Your shelter will leak when it rains.
Your gas will get shut off.
Your electricity too.
Your water will get shut off.
Your pregnant daughter will move in.
She'll lose the baby.
Bill collectors will call.
Your son will go to jail
and then on to prison.
This is a mobile home
but don't think
you're going anywhere.

The Cage

Someone has mounted a speaker in a wire cage
and attached it to the brick wall
twenty feet above the sidewalk
over the entrance to the downtown YMCA.
The cage is sturdy, though badly dented
from rocks and bottles thrown
in attempts to stop the 24/7
classical music broadcast at high volume
to deter loitering.

I enter the building.
Cigarettes, sweat and urine.
All surfaces smooth:
vinyl and plastic seating to facilitate
easy cleanup of bodily fluids.
I'm buzzed through a series of doors
to the elevator. Hit 6 for Sam's room.

I'm here for my annual follow-up.
Sam's in a good mood.
Better than last year,
when the only word he uttered was
Why?
We both know the routine.
I ask the questions and Sam answers.
Yes, he's doing fine.
Yes, he's clean, going to his meetings.
I'm out in five minutes,
with a promise to return in one year.

Sometimes it gets to me.
How do people live this way?
Why don't they shut this place down?
Seven floors of eighty rooms.
Five hundred sixty Sams.

Outside, a woman is wailing in Italian
from the caged speaker.

A guy in dreadlocks, dirty white Nikes,
claps his hands over his ears,
looks for something to throw.

Luxury

Still somewhat drunk
from the night before, I retain enough sense
to pour the maggot from my microwaved coffee
down the kitchen sink.

The question of how it got there
remains unanswered several minutes
after thorough search of microwave,
coffee pot, countertops.

I pour another cup, ponder the question of eggs.
I've got a two-hundred-mile drive
to Cleveland this morning
to repair a broken tooth.

On the bright side I've got a Subaru
that always starts and a good CD collection.
I'm in the mood for a long slow Dylan song,
sit in the middle lane on cruise control at 75,
let cars whiz by on either side.

Medicare says we can do without teeth,
which they label as "luxury items" along
with our eyes. Private pay remains an option,
so I pay a thin man with thinning
hair nine hundred dollars to
torture me, then thank him.

One of life's pleasures is my fully stocked bar.
That's what I'll think about
driving home from Cleveland with a throbbing jaw,
Dylan intoning "It's not dark yet but it's getting there."

Jerry and Amy

Jerry was never without Amy.
They looked alike with matching
Farrah Fawcett hairdos.
I mistook them for brother and sister.
Amy on the handlebars of Jerry's ten speed
as they rode to and from school,
as they played tennis with white shorts,
headbands and a look of privilege.
Jerry and Amy had beautiful smiles,
perfect white teeth.

But there was something wrong.
I asked them one night
at a keg party if they were
brother and sister. A strange look
came over Jerry's face and he
tried to kiss Amy in a way
to put an end to the question.

After the kiss
we stood there,
Jerry behind Amy with his hands
jammed into the front pockets of Amy's jeans.
I filled a red plastic cup
with foamy beer and walked away.

A few days later I saw them
riding their bike again.
Amy perched on the handlebars,
smiling at something
Jerry said.
I watched them
from my second story window
wondering
if something was wrong
with them
or me.

Little Phrase from Brahms

I see my mother,
violin tucked under chin,
starting the same phrase from Brahms
over and over again.
Her desperation making a terrible music
on a cheap instrument pressed together in Gary, Indiana
with a crack in the seam where the back meets the side.

No amount of glue,
clamps or forty thousand repetitions
could make it sing like Heifetz or Perlman.

If it's not in the fingers and wires,
the burning horsehair, or your own locks
flopping over your forehead in the wild passages,
it's not there. Possession, blind ambition,
jealousy of all those who came before.

She didn't know the need of Heifetz,
bow burning.
Perlman with his bad legs,
willing to die for it –
even that little phrase from Brahms.

Leonard and I

were breaking into vans,
searching for dope when
two squids burst from the parking lot,
chased us across 3rd Street.
I jumped the fence into
some old lady's flower garden,
flattened out and prayed
she didn't have a dog.
All quiet but the squids
beating feet down 17th
after Leonard who made it
all the way back to Geno's,
where we emptied our pockets:
a dime bag of Mexican and two
blue valiums. Leonard got crazy
on a pint of Jim Beam we split,
got me in a headlock. We went
round and round on the linoleum
until I found the empty pint,
cracked him on the head.
The bottle broke, cut my hand,
Leonard from temple to nose.
My hand healed. Leonard
kept the scar. We were
buddies like that for years.

Pareidolia

Now is the time to sit in my white plastic chair
on the patio, light my cigarette and
let it kill me.
I look up through slats of the pergola
at a black December sky,
thinking of blind ambition,
the regions of the mind it fires,
and how I'm done with that.
A bare branch against the white face of the moon
is more interesting.
Scrape, hiss, flare of a wooden match.

It's difficult to make faces out of clouds at night
but I see them.
So quiet
I light another match
for the hiss.
The face of God appears,
yellow as the sun.
It dies, but not
before burning.

Waiting for faces to appear.
To flare in a match, a branch,
a cloud of smoke moving over
the pocked face of the moon.

Wolf Circles the Dream

Nineteen below zero as I smoke
a hand-rolled cigarette,
back to the wind in my Russian coat.
Return to the warm house,
somebody's bebop punctuating the stillness.
Piano against back wall
containing no wrong notes,
half inch of dust.

I think of the wolf tonight
as I sip Wild Turkey over ice.
All he possesses is his skin.
Warmth, whiskey, jazz......
and I'm the one who envies
the wolf his eyes.

Blame it on the gradual elimination
of manual labor. The wolf
seems to be smiling as he circles the fire,
but he's easily misunderstood.
It's official. There are no more
undiscovered Indians.
They all want in on the dream.

Juniper Jones

I killed the ignition, stepped into CVS
for candy, antibiotics and beer.
Earlier in the day, a street musician told me
when he got to heaven he was going
to beat the shit out of God.
Everything was going to hell,
the flowers were dying,
someone stole his straightjacket,
his head was his only home.
Nails jammed with dirt,
tears, the temperature of life,
flew off his face. I was wishing
wide water washing away.
But I stopped to pay him,
playing like a cross between
John Lee Hooker and Beethoven.
Said he was born in Gothic, Colorado
to a fellow named Mingo Fishtrap,
but that wasn't the name he took.
His mother caught a heart attack.
He drank nothing stronger than milk and
ginger ale, no matter what I thought. He said
your heart looks colder than a well-digger's ass.
I gave him a dollar, an accurate silence.
He said his name was Juniper Jones,
no matter what I thought.

Giant

At the age of thirty Patrick Macklamore
had reached the height of eight foot two.
The only man I ever met who admitted
he had no sense of humor. Claimed it was
beaten out of him at the age of two.
Hated flowers, hummingbirds and
the sound of wind chimes. Traveled
the southern circuit with the King
Brothers Circus, doubling as a geek
when Brad was ill. Lived in constant
pain due to twenty-seven chronic
diseases, including opiate addiction.
Carried a vial of morphine sulfate
in a suitcase that looked like a toy
in his hand. We tied off. Took him
ten minutes to find a vein. There was
no radio in his trailer, said he hated
music. Just the roar of the air
conditioner and a tiny black and white
television with faulty vertical hold.
Got out a photo album of his
normal sized parents, his mother
who died giving birth to Patrick,
his father who never forgave him.
When the words dried up
we listened to a fly buzz
in the window pane, Pat's asthma.
Then I got in my Dodge and the King
Brothers Circus left town.

quaaludes and cuervo

dave had injected something and was
screaming from the house next door.
whatever it was i wanted it
but i couldn't walk and the
screaming wouldn't stop because
we had no windows in the beach
house no glass in windows I mean.
it was quaaludes and cuervo
had me laid out and fearless.
dave's bleached hut had
the house of the rising sun
painted on in pink. he'd
calmed down by then and
i had my senses back and the
bottle of cuervo we passed
around to hendrix on loud.
beat my hands so hard as
percussion instruments on the
chair arms next morning thought
someone had run them over.
when i woke in the oyster shell
parking lot they told me
it wasn't true.

Nadine

Nadine was a blackout drunk
who kissed ferociously after half a bottle of wine.
She had small hard eyes and a face
not spoiled by beauty. Smelled of
kerosene and cat piss. Sold electric sugar
from a flatbed beneath the bridge. Told me
she was born the day the music died.

We headed west through heavy weather,
lived all summer off red squirrel,
skunk cabbage, mudbank carp.
One morning I woke up in Cherokee, Iowa
with a bloody nose and half a headful of hair.
Nadine was good with a razor and strong as any man.
I must have made a noise getting up.
Her eyes slid open.

I got out of there like a bullet from a gun.
All I had were white lines heading east,
a pair of too tight shoes and a flash of
Nadine's eyes for the rest of my life,
sharp as a flick knife.
Rain was coming on.

Never Enough

I'm behind an old Ford Ranger
stacked twenty feet high with a
teetering pile of pallets, tailpipe belching
black exhaust, pancaked tires
wincing over potholes,
forty-five in the slow lane.

I pull out to pass, glance over at the driver.
Younger than I thought, wearing a
red ball cap and black beard,
star tattoo on left arm,
cigarette planted in right fist,
all windows down.

South of town, off 665, Merle's Recycle
displays a billboard offering
current prices for scrap metal:
45 cents for aluminum cans,
2.25 for copper wire,
1.20 for brass.

I don't know how much they pay for pallets,
but it's probably not enough.
When hard work is called for,
it's never enough.
Ranger in my rearview now,
headed south.

Tammy Wynette Blues

Thinking of Tammy Wynette,
I wake at five a.m. with the line
Your love is so blonde it makes a woman blue.
I have a melody and hear
steel guitar and piano fills.

Meanwhile, on TCM with the sound off,
Frankenstein is playing with daisies.
In a burst of irritation,
he throws a little girl down a well.
I think about going back to bed,
but it's seven a.m. and I'm filled with coffee.

I see the monster trapped in a burning windmill
surrounded by jeering villagers,
and it brings back the years
I used to go to bed
hoping not to wake up.

I don't live like Miss Tammy anymore.
She had beautiful hair and a mouth
full of vodka and pills.
Died young. Like what I was shooting for.

That didn't pan out.
The old movie's over.
My day's just beginning.
And I started a new song for Tammy.

Sixty

I always wanted to be old.
Now I'm granted permission.
Though I'm appalled
at the physical corruption.
More and more aware
I only feel better
when I feel no pain.

Never comfortable in my own skin,
but maybe a little more
now. No expectations. Freed
from the desire to prove anything,
I still avoid
the soul murder of mirrors.

I'm at best in my own thoughts.
But careful what you wish for,
I've found. The well
is full of pennies.

The Healer

I've always suspected it
but now I'm sure
I need some degree of
sadness in my life.
Most apparent in the music
I turn to when low.
Blues is the healer,
says John Lee Hooker.
A big glass of iced bourbon
and Charlie Haden's bass
tonight have healed me of the
21st century disease of digital ennui.
The sun still rises but hotter,
and I'll still wake and stare
into the screen I know on one level
is composed of ones and zeros,
for too many hours. But then
I'm not picking lettuce or strawberries
in the Napa Valley by the luck of the draw,
or rather my lack of melanin.
I'm listening to Charlie Haden
in my air-conditioned suburban home
with my bourbon and jazz
after feeling down and blue all day.
When the bourbon is gone I
eat the bourbon flavored ice.

Sodbuster

No one on my father's side
wanted to be a farmer.

From a family of twelve boys,
eleven left the farm.

Only Tom remained.

One became a sailor,
another a mechanic.

Three were drunks,
one a salesman of septic systems.

The youngest son became a pastor
in a small church
way out west.

Two played the saxophone
and one the ukulele.

Only Tom remained,
tied to earth.

I remember how he smiled,
chest out, high in the seat
of his manure spreader,

up to his eyes in debt.

Gentle on My Mind

Another friend has died of cancer –
Pancreatic. Three rounds of chemo.
We've reached the age where it's
always on our minds. Not gentle though.

John Hartford wrote that song,
not Glenn Campbell, who made it famous.
You can never go back, they say,
you can't repeat the past.
But I've lived there most of my life.

Thinking about Doug as I
fry three eggs, stir some oatmeal.
Doug only lasted nine months
after he retired from Ohio State.

I sit down to my breakfast and newspaper,
scan the obituaries.
I should go to the funeral
but I can't get off work.
Nobody can retire anymore,
it seems.

I'll go to my mind,
where everyone lives
forever and the songs
are so much better.

Stage Fright

I set my stage with red satin,
elevate my tweed Deluxe,
sing through a 1948 Shure Monoplex,
everything tube driven and lit from below
so shadows loom and waver
and the mood is right for blues.

Open with a bang and whisper,
keep them hanging from the purse of your lips,
inhale for drama. Use wood, wire and the
spark of Mr. Edison's invention.
My right thumb trembles on the bass string,
my left leg shakes but my throat opens
at full force. Always,

my suit is soaked and my hat is ringed.
What is this but joy and terror?
Hours later, left hand still clamped
around the shape of the microphone,
right around a cigarette,
buzz from the brain all the way
down to the toes every time.

Plasma

Always looking for a new place to be born,
escape from the smell of blood and flies,
Ray Bob, Joe Jack and I, meet at the blood bank.

Sticky weather, quiet as a snail.
Watching the red rag of a dog's tongue
across the street, waiting for the door to open.

Ray Bob never shows his teeth when he laughs.
Joe Jack rat-a-tats like a machine gun
over razor wire.

God went to sleep and we got born
wrong, half-baked and broken.
The door opens.

On tv, in the lobby,
the Life of Evel Knievel
with the sound off.

Ray Bob goes first, comes out rubbing.
Then Joe Jack, who mumbles something
about *mysterious manmade workings*.

We cross over to the liquor store,
next to Cuatro's Dentistry,
Teeth in a Day, Done the Right Way.

Then to our separate corners.
I hope it won't rain again.
The sky hangs like a judge.

Ray Bob can walk on his hands,
holds his sign in his teeth,
a small box of stars.

Joe Jack lost his marbles

at the Ohio State Fair,
started screaming on the Sky Liner.

I'm partial to gin in the morning,
sleep off the afternoon. Up all night
arguing with the dead, who won't let me in.

Winter Solstice

Nothing wrong with a little tobacco
if used properly,
the lie I tell myself.
A touch of the poppy
now and then.
Red wine is good for you.
Have a glass with your evening meal.
Some people can do that:
the fit and trim,
sophisticated connoisseurs.
What a world of difference
between them and winos
beneath the overpass
who prefer fortified wine
for the alcohol content.

And where do I fit into the equation,
with my bottle of Russian Imperial Stout
and fifth of tequila?
I won't stop at one beer,
that's for sure.
I won't take two Vicodin
and call it a night.

I'm floating somewhere between
the junkie, the wino and the poet.
That's my reality tonight,
with a lower right molar
that probably needs a root canal,
my twenty-year
addiction to opiates.

The stars are out on this clear night
as I smoke my hand-rolled American Spirit cigarette.
The wino, the connoisseur and I
all looking for the good life.

He Swears He Sees

Our story starts with the oysterboy
in the church of the wrong-eyed Jesus.
Blowing his horn so badly,
feeding the burning bush
spades of napalm
with a plastic shovel.
The oysterboy molded by the shell
he shucks behind the scenes,
against the grain,
beneath the false floor
where the screams are buried.
The strangles burst like bubbles from the bell,
the boy bent with total permanent embolism.
The cries of the pew-squatters never pierce
his ears, his pleasures never sweeter
than the grave he daily craves.
He swears he sees milk and stars
when he plays, god with aqua-vivid eyes.
He turns himself into a stranger
when he plays "Harney Basin Blues,"
"Master Of Emptiness" with a sugared brain
so slow the bugs begin to walk,
the mouse begins to roar.
He wakes up with the staggers and the jags,
struggles through the quickmud,
sees the closed door open, the clock hands go back.
When he sees he plays his brains off,
blows his lip out, bleeds his gums dry,
down in burning hog oil he swears
he sees way out past the milk and stars.

McClenney to Beeville

I step outside for the night's last cigarette.
So quiet I hear paper,
tobacco sizzle the permanent scar
between my first and second fingers.

I think about my old friend Leonard Larson.
Leonard had a broad, angry brow
like his hero Beethoven.
Compared his mastery of harmonica
to Beethoven's command of piano.
Several years of failing to convince
anyone of this, and a dual diagnosis,
got him sent away to the horrors of McClenney
for six months of ECT and a lifetime of Thorazine.

I drove a Kenworth for forty years,
then a bottle of Wild Turkey deep into the night.
Ended up in a trailer east of Beeville, Texas.
So quiet I hear paper
burn, flesh sizzle.
Not sure what got me thinking of
Leonard again, but he
would have liked it here.
Maybe it's the peace and quiet.

To the north, an orange moon
cracks like an egg on the mountain.
It was never quiet in McClenney,
Leonard confessed.

I finish my cigarette,
watch the yolk run down
the other side of the mountain.

Buttermilk Johnson

With sugared brain and oxygen tank
the old blues man staggered across the stage,
plugged in and turned to face
ten thousand eyes, cheers, whistles,
waves on waves of love.
In sharp suit with sweet tooth
he goldly grinned. *Where were you
fifty years ago? All my life
most things haven't worked out.
I'm a bad motherfucker!*
The love crowd swelled and wowed
to every wrist flick, every pick pinch
from thumb to pinky. Sting and burn,
snare crack, harp moan, the old man
in shiny shoes sweated through his hat band.
His rings caught light, flashed and fired.
He woke this morning with the staggers and the jags,
wished he would have woke up dead.

*Look at them out there,
they don't even know my name.*
The old man tethered by tubes
to oxygen, cable to boom box, moved
back into the shadows, made it weep,
made it sting. *They don't know
my favorite word's goodbye.*

Paychecks and Fish Heads

The sad clown and the black bear
tire of their roles, but continue
for paychecks and fish heads.
Center stage, the two
strum ukuleles, the bear's
singing slightly less mournful.

The keepers slap a muzzle on,
pull his claws, watch him waltz
and wobble with neighborhood wrestlers,
ten dollars a pop.

The clown's name is Herbert,
the bear is Joe Jack. He's afraid
of the electric prod.
Remembers the day it killed his mother.
Though toothless, she managed to
end her tormentor's life
with one last lunge and maul.

Herbert married and divorced
four times before the age of thirty.
He's two years younger than Joe Jack
but looks older.
Joe Jack's bicycle is custom made,
painted blue with gold stars,
large leather seat, straps on pedals
to buckle his paws in.

Herbert buys his own makeup
and fright wigs. Clown suit
gone shiny in the seat.
Two pair of shoes to his name,
one too large, one too small.

Friday nights, Herbert collects $95.
Joe Jack roars with joy
for herring and a bucket of blackberries.

The clown prefers gin and tonic,
roars when drunk
but rarely with joy.

Late Winter Blues

Bucks rubbed the oak saplings shiny
marking their territory this winter.
It's cold and windy but daffodils
push through snow, cherry trees
pop pale pink petals.
It's the time of year I vow
to shed my dead skin, when does starve,
when a wild turkey attacks
an animal control officer in Hilliard, Ohio
and has to be removed to the country.

I'm watching a desperate cardinal
breaking his beak against a garden globe
in the front yard.
I'd like to save him,
but I know a tape loop
runs through his brain vowing
I'll have his blood or he'll have mine.

On tv, with the sound off,
a gothic shoegazer mimes his misery
with black lips and milk white face.

I return to the window.
Remember the daffodil was well known as
Hitler's favorite flower.

I see a future of ethical billionaires,
tattooed politicians, corpse-colored clouds.
Fingers wrapped around a
tumbler of cask strength bourbon,
I need to shed this dead skin before
the shotgun in the basement
turns my head into oatmeal.

Sizzler

Sharp of tongue and mind at eighty-five,
work shirt darkened with axle grease,
"Jimmy" patched over the left breast pocket,
my grandfather bites off
half a raw green onion
at the Sizzler in Springfield, Ohio.
He eats there once a day,
all he can stomach,
then sleeps it off.

The other side of the family
has banished him from gatherings
for some unspeakable sin
many years ago.

I know him
as the only man to scare my father.
Even now, scolding Dad
for some lapse in judgement,
as we sit at the table.
Three hearts racing
for three different reasons.

It's Raining at the Birthplace of Ulysses S. Grant

This is not Grant's Tomb, but it could have been.
This is Grant's birthplace: Southern Ohio,
between Portsmouth and Cincinnati.
This is April and Flowering Dogwood is in bloom,
white and pink petals against green hills,
cows grazing on bloodwort and stinkweed.

It's raining at four o'clock in the afternoon
and the cocoon of the webworm beads up,
caterpillars reaching forward in wet air.
Nothing new has been born here since
hillbilly heroin, oxytots in daycare.
This is not Grant's Tomb, but it could have been.

Moonshine stills, meth labs,
pregnant grandmothers, predator priests.
The webworm in the crotch of the dogwood
is killing the tree. The caterpillars
reach out to move forward.
Raindrops knock the weaker ones down.

Late Night Poem

I don't know what time it is,
nicotine lacing its spell through
blood with cask strength bourbon,
mind still ticking despite decades of damage.

I predict the '20's will be good to me
though possibly fatal.
I'm betting on the muse
to carry me onward into uncertainty.
Nothing given but the tunnel
at the end of the light.

One last cigarette before I return
to the house to warm up.
Whir of wheel against flint,
draw of hot smoke through lips.
The cigarette burns the permanent scar
between fingers. I listen to it
sizzle. It hurts a little
to be alive.

Open Mic

I met him at a poetry reading
in a bowling alley in Youngstown, Ohio.
He introduced himself as a volleyball player
with a sixty-inch vertical leap.
Said he could run faster than dogs
and most cars,
as long as it was short distance.

It was a hot night in September,
and I remember almost everything
he told me, except for his name,
which was either Jim or Joe.
I'll go with Joe.

A hemophiliac skydiver raised by wolves
and hippies in communes all across the country.
His ship in a bottle on display at the Smithsonian
after being recommended by JFK's mother, Rose,
who was lonely one afternoon
and invited him into the house to talk.
He was, at one time, an insurance salesman,
and for a brief period, vice president of Waffle House.

Sexually insatiable as a young man,
he was now impotent from anti-psychotics.
He'd done some time, but swore
he never touched the girl.
He was sixty-seven years old.
He was a bouncer at a strip club,
in love with a twenty-one year old dancer
named Crystal, who loved him back.

I thought he was full of shit
until he cried at the open mic
reading a poem about his father.
Then I saw his skinny legs in his
huge cargo shorts stuffed with notebooks,

wallet, cell phone, cigarettes, gum,
lighter, knife, everything he had.
His poem about his father was the best of the night.

The reading ended when a band named
Milk & Stars took the stage at 11:00.
I tried to catch him in the parking lot
but he was gone.
Just a garbage can tipped over,
possum crawling out.
Everything on earth is true,
said Joe. He was hard to follow.

Crepuscule with Bourbon and Cigar

On the patio, smoking a cheap cigar,
sipping Wild Turkey over ice.
8:00 pm, eighty degrees,
slapping my first mosquito of the season.
I spent the first half of my day at the office,
grinding my mental teeth.
But last light falling through cottonwood
lights a pink peony in a white vase.
I think of late October,
when I was last out here,
hornets drunk and dying,
crawling over falls,
the long sodden winter that followed.

I'll die some night of no regret,
but not this one. Clematis climbing
up red cedar fence.
Ice cubes melting in bourbon.
Sun sinking lower by degree.
My first tobacco in three years,
and the nightjar swoops over the
darkening sky.

How wonderful to be
old at last, nothing to prove,
most of the anger washed away.
I can barely see the white contrail
of a jet disappearing in the west.

Acknowledgments

Some of the poems in this collection have appeared in or are forthcoming in the following journals:

A Gathering Of The Tribes: "Blind Faith," "He Swears He Sees"; *Abbey*: "Little Phrase From Brahms"; *California Quarterly*: "Wolf Circles The Dream"; *Cheap Seats*: "hootenanny"; *Children, Churches & Daddies*: "Open Mic"; *Coal City Review*: "Half Past December," "Giant," "Paychecks And Fish Heads," "quaaludes and cuervo"; *Common Threads*: "Pareidolia"; *Floyd County Moonshine*: "Crepuscule With Bourbon And Cigar," "Kinship," "Late Night Poem," "Nadine," "Osmosis,"; *Home Planet News*: "Hawk and Cop," "Plasma," "Winter Solstice" "Youth"; *Iconoclast*: "Sodbuster," "Still Preying"; *Lake Effect*: "Empty Rooms," "Stroke Dance"; *Lipsmack! 2016 Anthology*: "Graveyard Shift"; *Nerve Cowboy*: "Never Enough"; *POEM*: "Stage Fright"; *Pennsylvania English*: "Gravel Road"; *Pudding Magazine*: "Celebration," "It's Raining At The Birthplace Of Ulysses S. Grant," "Swineherd"; *Red River Review*: "Just Visiting"; *San Pedro River Review*: "The Healer"; *Ship Of Fools*: "Jerry And Amy"; *Straylight Literary Magazine*: "Juniper Jones"; *The Avalon Literary Review*: "Sixty," "Sizzler"; *The Comstock Review*: "Mechanic"; *The Listening Eye*: "Buttermilk Johnson," "IH"; *The Midwest Quarterly*: "Diagnosis," "Leaning Toward Greenland," "Obituaries Over Coffee"; *Third Wednesday*: "The Cage," "Gentle On My Mind," "Mobile Home"; *Thorny Locust*: "Leonard And I"; *US1 Worksheets*: "Parsimony," "Seized By The Notion," "Tammy Wynette Blues"; *Willow Review*: "Child Bride"

Cover: Jean Pillement, *A Shipwreck in a Storm,* ca. 1782

www.ingramcontent.com/pod-product-compliance
Lightning Source LLC
Chambersburg PA
CBHW051707090426
42736CB00013B/2577